STO 6/06

ACPL I P9-EDI-965

DISCARDED

THE SOLAR SYSTEM

EARTH

A MyReportLinks.com Book

STEPHEN FEINSTEIN

MyReportLinks.com Books

an imprint of

 Enslow Publishers, Inc.

Box 398, 40 Industrial Road
Berkeley Heights, NJ 07922
USA

MyReportLinks.com Books, an imprint of Enslow Publishers, Inc. MyReportLinks® is a registered trademark of Enslow Publishers, Inc.

Copyright © 2005 by Enslow Publishers, Inc.

All rights reserved.

No part of this book may be reproduced by any means without the written permission of the publisher.

Library of Congress Cataloging-in-Publication Data

Feinstein, Stephen.
  Earth / Stephen Feinstein.
    p. cm. — (The solar system)
  Includes bibliographical references and index.
  ISBN 0-7660-5301-6
  1. Earth—Juvenile literature. I. Title. II. Solar system (Berkeley Heights, N.J.)
  QB631.4.F45 2005
  525—dc22

                            2004008324

Printed in the United States of America

10 9 8 7 6 5 4 3 2 1

To Our Readers:
Through the purchase of this book, you and your library gain access to the Report Links that specifically back up this book.

The Publisher will provide access to the Report Links that back up this book and will keep these Report Links up to date on **www.myreportlinks.com** for five years from the book's first publication date.

We have done our best to make sure all Internet addresses in this book were active and appropriate when we went to press. However, the author and the Publisher have no control over, and assume no liability for, the material available on those Internet sites or on other Web sites they may link to.

The usage of the MyReportLinks.com Books Web site is subject to the terms and conditions stated on the Usage Policy Statement on **www.myreportlinks.com**.

A password may be required to access the Report Links that back up this book. The password is found on the bottom of page 4 of this book.

Any comments or suggestions can be sent by e-mail to comments@myreportlinks.com or to the address on the back cover.

Photo Credits: © Corel Corporation, pp. 15, 25, 38, 39, 41, 43; © PBS, p. 37; © PhotoDisc, Inc., p. 10; © Windows to the Universe, p. 29; Enslow Publishers, Inc., p. 32; High Altitude Observatory, p. 13; MyReportLinks.com Books, p. 4; National Aeronautics and Space Administration (NASA), pp. 1, 3, 9, 12, 16, 26; National Oceanic and Atmospheric Administration (NOAA), p. 35; Oceansonline.com, p. 18; Online Journey Through Astronomy, pp. 28, 31; Photos.com, pp. 3, 9, 36; United States Geological Survey, pp. 19, 21, 22.

Cover Photo: National Aeronautics and Space Administration

Report Links **4**

Earth Facts **9**

1 **The Home Planet** **10**

2 **A Planet of Constant Change** **15**

3 **Earth's Oceans and Atmosphere** **24**

4 **Revolution and Rotation** **29**

5 **Life on Earth** **34**

Glossary **45**

Chapter Notes **46**

Further Reading **47**

Index **48**

MyReportLinks.com Books
Great Books, Great Links, Great for Research!

The Internet sites listed on the next four pages can save you hours of research time. These Internet sites—we call them "Report Links"—are constantly changing, but we keep them up to date on our Web site.

Give it a try! Type http://www.myreportlinks.com into your browser, click on the series title, then the book title, and scroll down to the Report Links listed for this book.

The Report Links will bring you to great source documents, photographs, and illustrations. MyReportLinks.com Books save you time, feature Report Links that are kept up to date, and make report writing easier than ever!

Please see "To Our Readers" on the copyright page for important information about this book, the MyReportLinks.com Web site, and the Report Links that back up this book.

Please enter **PEA1549** if asked for a password.

Report Links

The Internet sites described below can be accessed at
http://www.myreportlinks.com

*EDITOR'S CHOICE

▶**Exploring The Planets: Earth**
By using specialized space satellites and sensors, scientists gather a large amount of data about Earth much easier and much more quickly than they can from the ground. At this site, learn about some of the technology involved.

*EDITOR'S CHOICE

▶**Earth From Space**
What do astronauts see from space? Can they see a hurricane forming, pollution, or deforestation? You can now search NASA's Space Shuttle Earth Observations Photography database for images of Earth taken by astronauts in space.

*EDITOR'S CHOICE

▶**NASA Earth Observatory**
The site has sections on Earth's atmosphere, oceans, land, energy, and living things and includes images of Earth. You can even ask a NASA scientist a question through an e-mail form.

*EDITOR'S CHOICE

▶**Earth**
This site presents an overview of Planet Earth, including its layers, tectonic plates, atmosphere, chemical composition, and magnetic field.

*EDITOR'S CHOICE

▶**The Earth's Atmosphere**
Earth's atmosphere is made up of four layers: the troposphere, the stratosphere (containing the ozone layer), the mesosphere, and the ionosphere. This site offers a description and images of each layer.

*EDITOR'S CHOICE

▶**NASA Oceanography**
NASA Oceanography is a division of the space agency that conducts satellite missions to observe the state and patterns of change in Earth's oceans. At this site, learn more about the connection between the oceans and our climate.

Report Links

The Internet sites described below can be accessed at http://www.myreportlinks.com

▶ The Cambrian Period

The first groups of animals first appear in the fossil record from the Cambrian Period in Earth's history. This site offers a look at the "explosion of life" on Earth that occurred relatively quickly.

▶ Continental Drift

Alfred Wegener, a German scientist, was the first person in modern times to provide compelling evidence for the theory of continental drift. This site offers a brief overview of Wegener's theory and drawings that illustrate his theory.

▶ Did Plants Cool the Earth and Spark Explosion of Life?

Scientists at Pennsylvania State University say it was plants that gave animal species a jump start and colonized Earth much earlier than we realize. This article questions whether plants were really on Earth that long ago.

▶ Earth and Habitat

This PBS site offers links to sites on a wide variety of subjects, including oceans, weather systems, nature, and science. Test yourself with interactive quizzes and trivia games.

▶ The Earth's Atmosphere: Near Real-Time Research Imagery

Predicting Earth's weather patterns is a difficult task but one made easier by the use of satellites. This NASA site examines the advances in weather-satellite technology since the 1960s.

▶ Eratosthenes

At this Web site from PBS, you can read a brief biography of the Greek astronomer Eratosthenes. About 230 B.C., he became the first person to accurately calculate the circumference of Earth.

▶ Evolution: Humans

This Web site, based on the PBS series, explores the changes in life that have taken place throughout Earth's history. Photographs and descriptions of the fossils of early humans are included.

▶ Find by Interest: Earth

This PBS site is a portal, or entryway, to topics about Earth, including global warming, fire, ice ages, weather, volcanoes, floods, glaciers, caves, and more.

Report Links

▶ **For Kids Only—Earth Science Enterprise**

This NASA site for children puts together information on air, thunderstorms, Earth's crust, tropical storms, earthquakes, and much more. You can even send an electronic postcard from the site.

▶ **The Gaia Hypothesis**

In 1979, British scientist James Lovelock proposed that Earth is a living organism that provides all it needs to sustain itself. This site takes a look at his controversial "Gaia Hypothesis."

▶ **Historical Views of Our Solar System**

For millennia, people believed that Earth was the center of the universe and everything else in space, including the Sun, revolved around it. This site discusses that theory, the geocentric theory, and early astronomers who opposed it.

▶ **Inside the Earth**

Earth is made up of three layers: the crust, mantle, and core. This Web site from the United States Geological Survey examines Earth's layers.

▶ **Johannes Kepler**

Read about the German astronomer who helped change our understanding of the solar system and our planet's place in it. Links to related topics and an image of Kepler are included in this site.

▶ **Journey to Planet Earth**

Seven PBS programs that examine the relationship we humans have with our planet are accessed through this site. Vivid photographs accompany the text.

▶ **The Milky Way Galaxy**

Earth is just one planet in our solar system, which itself is part of the huge Milky Way galaxy. At this site, find out about the giant spiral galaxy we are part of and follow links for images and a lot more information.

▶ **National Oceanic and Atmospheric Administration (NOAA)**

The National Oceanic and Atmospheric Administration, or NOAA, is a government agency that conducts research in oceanography and related subjects. Its Web site includes images of Earth's oceans and marine life.

Report Links

The Internet sites described below can be accessed at http://www.myreportlinks.com

▶**Satellites**

This NASA site takes a look at satellites in space, which provide voice and data communications, make weather forecasting more accurate, produce military surveillance, determine location and navigation, and more.

▶**The Solar System**

We now know a lot more about our solar system and how it works than people did as recently as fifty years ago. At this site, read about the history of astronomy.

▶**The Theory of Plate Tectonics**

This site examines the theory of plate tectonics, which states that Earth's outer layer is made up of large slabs of rocks called plates that have moved throughout history. Their shifting has created mountains, volcanoes, and earthquakes, among other things.

▶**This Dynamic Earth: The Story of Plate Tectonics**

The plate tectonics theory caused a revolution in scientific thought and research. Learn more about this theory and its impact at this site.

▶**Welcome to the Planets: Earth**

On this NASA Web site, you can view three pages of images of Earth and the Moon with descriptions. The images come with a zoom feature, and terms are explained in a glossary.

▶**What Causes Earth to Experience Different Seasons?**

On this site, learn why we experience different seasons on Earth. A diagram shows where Earth is relative to the Sun during the spring, summer, fall, and winter months.

▶**What Went On Before the Breakup of Pangaea?**

The landmasses on Earth that we know as continents were once joined as a "supercontinent" called Pangaea. This government site speculates on what Earth was like before the continents were separate.

▶**World Builders: Introduction to Biomes**

Biomes are areas on Earth that support specific climates, plants, and animals. This site, recommended by teachers of science, examines six biomes found on Earth and the interrelationships between the living things in each.

Earth Facts

Age
About 4.6 billion years

Diameter
7,926 miles (12,760 kilometers)

Composition
Core—solid iron and nickel; outer part is molten, or liquefied by heat

Mantle—mostly solid rock; outer part is semiliquid

Crust—various kinds of rock and soil

Atmosphere
78 percent nitrogen, 20 percent oxygen, 1 percent argon, 1 percent water vapor

Distance From the Sun
About 93 million miles (150 million kilometers)

Orbital Period
365 days 6 hours

Rotational Period
24 hours (23 hours 56 minutes)

Temperature Range
Coldest: −128°F (−90°C) in parts of Antarctica

Warmest: 120°F (50°C) in parts of Australia and Africa

Number of Moons
One

Greatest Ocean Depth
Mariana Trench, in the Pacific Ocean, 36,198 feet (11,033 meters) deep

Highest Mountain
Mount Everest, in Nepal and Tibet, 29,035 feet (8,850 meters) high

Lowest Point
Dead Sea, in Israel and Jordan, 1,349 feet (411 meters) below sea level

Land Area
57,308,738 square miles (148,429,545 square kilometers)

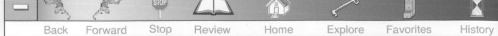
The Home Planet

Earth, the third planet from the Sun in our solar system, was formed about 4.6 billion years ago. One of the nine planets in the solar system, it is the only one we know of where living things—plants, animals, and people—can exist. Earth is a terrestrial planet, composed of rock and metal. *Terra* is Greek for "earth," and the term *terrestrial* is used to refer to our planet and three other planets, Mercury, Venus, and Mars, that are like Earth in the materials they are made of. All terrestrial planets except Mercury have an atmosphere, but Earth's atmosphere is the only one that has allowed life to form and continue.

3 1833 05019 0252

▲ *While Earth is the only planet we know of that supports life, people continue to gaze at the sky and wonder what other worlds might hold.*

While Venus and Mars may once have had oceans, Earth is now the only body in the solar system with liquid water on its surface. More than 70 percent of Earth's surface is covered by water, in the form of oceans. Water is essential for Earth's unique characteristic—the presence of life, an amazing diversity of living organisms including us.

Astronomers in recent years have discovered planets revolving around distant stars. These planets are giant gaseous bodies bearing no resemblance to Earth. But that does not mean that planets like Earth do not exist in other parts of the galaxy. It is just that we do not yet have powerful enough telescopes to detect bodies as small as Earth that are so far away.

A Pale Blue Dot

Because Earth is our home, we sometimes tend to think of it as the most important planet in the solar system. When viewed as part of the "big picture" of the universe, however, Earth is only a tiny speck of a planet revolving around a quite ordinary star, the Sun. Of course, that star makes life on Earth possible, but the Sun is only one star out of hundreds of billions of stars in the Milky Way galaxy. And the Milky Way is just one galaxy out of billions of galaxies, each having billions of stars. Describing our planet's place in the universe, astronomer Carl Sagan referred to Earth as a "pale blue dot."[1]

The Center of the Universe

Throughout much of human history, people believed that Earth was the center of the universe, or even that Earth "was" the universe. To ancient peoples, all the heavenly bodies that could be seen—the Sun, Moon, stars, and planets—were relatively near and revolved around Earth, which they believed was flat. Many considered these heavenly bodies to be gods or at least associated them with the gods. To the ancients, stars and planets spent their days

▲ *Crew members aboard the space shuttle* Discovery *took this image of sunlight over a cloud-covered Earth in March 1989.*

in the Underworld, and the Sun disappeared into the Underworld each night.

These beliefs by people who lived long ago cannot really be faulted, since they were based upon their observations and seemed to make sense. For them, Earth was motionless, while anybody could see that the Sun, Moon, planets, and stars rose and set each day. As astronomers learned more about the heavens, a few brilliant individuals came up with theories that challenged longstanding beliefs about the universe.

In ancient Greece, in about 270 B.C., the philosopher Aristarchus of Samos estimated that the Sun was much greater in size than Earth. He concluded from this that Earth and the other planets revolved around the Sun rather than the planets and the Sun revolving around Earth. He also believed that the stars were very, very far away. Aristarchus' theory of a solar system with the Sun at its center challenged the accepted theory. But most philosophers and astronomers at the time—and for nearly the next 1,900 years—did not accept Aristarchus' theory, since it went against common sense and the religious and philosophical views of the time.

The Man Who Measured the World

Around 230 B.C., the Greek astronomer Eratosthenes became the first person to measure Earth. Believing Earth to be round rather than flat, Eratosthenes used geometric calculations based on the

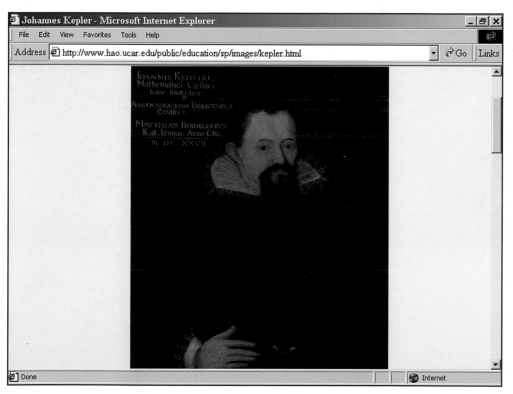

▲ *In the early seventeenth century, astronomer and mathematician Johannes Kepler proved that the planets, including Earth, revolved around the Sun in elliptical orbits. In addition to his scientific writings, Kepler is credited by some with writing the first science-fiction novel, which was published after his death. It described a voyage to the Moon.*

position of the Sun to estimate the distance around Earth, or its circumference. His figure of 25,000 miles was amazingly accurate: The actual figure is 24,900 miles. So the Greeks became fairly sure that Earth was round, but they still believed it was at the center of the universe. Ptolemy, a second-century A.D. Greek astronomer, continued that belief in his writings.

Ptolemy's view prevailed until 1543. That year, Polish astronomer Nicolaus Copernicus published *On the Revolutions of the Heavenly Spheres (or Bodies)*. In it, he argued that Earth was a planet like Mercury, Venus, Mars, Jupiter, and Saturn (the known planets at the time), and that all the planets revolved around a motionless Sun. Copernicus knew about Aristarchus' theory and agreed with the ancient Greek philosopher's ideas.

One of the strongest supporters of Copernicus' theory was a German astronomer, Johannes Kepler. In the early 1600s, Kepler proved that Copernicus' sun-centered model of the universe was correct, and he discovered that the planets moved around the Sun in elliptical orbits rather than in perfect circles. Kepler clearly understood why the view of Earth as the center of the universe had lasted so long. He wrote, "It is therefore impossible that reason not previously instructed should imagine anything other than that the Earth is a kind of vast house with the vault of the sky placed on top of it; it is motionless and within it the Sun being so small passes from one region to another, like a bird wandering through the air."[2]

Since Kepler's time, astronomers have been able to develop a more accurate picture of Earth's place in the universe by studying the heavens. Other scientists have used geological evidence, from Earth's surface and underground, to understand the structure of our planet and to try to learn how Earth was formed in the first place.

Chapter 2 ▶

A Planet of Constant Change

Earth has gone through enormous changes since its birth more than 4 billion years ago. Earthquakes and volcanoes have violently and suddenly changed the planet's surface. Earth's landmasses have also been eroded, or worn away, by the forces of wind, water, and moving glaciers. Continents that were once connected have split apart and drifted, mountain ranges have come and gone, and the oceans have risen and fallen in depth. Earth's atmosphere has also changed over time. As living organisms have evolved on Earth, they

▲ Volcanoes like this one, Kilauea, on the island of Hawaii, have changed the surface of Earth over time. Kilauea has erupted thirty-four times since the 1950s, making it one of the most active volcanoes on Earth.

too affected and were affected by the physical characteristics of the planet.

How Earth Was Formed

Most scientists believe that our solar system began to form about 4.6 billion years ago. The force of gravity pulled together hydrogen gas and dust particles floating in the space between stars into a spinning disk. The Sun formed first at the center of the disk. Then the planets formed out of dust and clumps of rocky debris circling the Sun.

The infant Earth grew larger as its gravitational pull scooped up rocks and specks of dust that crossed its orbital path. As Earth grew larger, it became hotter, causing the rocky material to melt and separate. The heavier elements, iron and nickel, sank to Earth's center and became the planet's core. Other materials

▲ The Moon, Earth's closest neighbor, appears to hover over Earth in this NASA photograph. The Moon's gravitational forces are responsible for the tides in Earth's oceans.

moved outward to form the mantle or rose to the planet's surface to form Earth's crust. Over millions of years, as Earth cooled, its atmosphere formed from volcanic gases, such as hydrogen, nitrogen, carbon dioxide, and water vapor, that were released from its hot interior. As the amount of water vapor increased, it began to fall to Earth in the form of rain. After millions of years, enough rain had fallen to create Earth's oceans. The water in these oceans helped to stabilize the temperature on Earth and allowed life to form and thrive.

How the Moon Was Formed

During the time it took Earth to form, it was bombarded by rocky bodies. One scientific theory, known as the Giant-Impact Theory, states that near the end of the process, a body as large as the planet Mars—and about half the size of Earth—smashed into our planet. The collision threw up a ring of debris that circled Earth, and about half of this debris came together to form the Moon, which is referred to as a satellite since it orbits our planet. Other planet's satellites are also referred to as moons, after our Moon.

The bombardment of Earth and the Moon by these bodies ended about 3.9 billion years ago. Evidence of the bombardment is plainly visible on the Moon's surface. Because the Moon has no atmosphere or oceans, its surface features have not eroded as Earth's have. By studying the Moon's large impact basins and craters, scientists can get a good idea of what must also have occurred on Earth during its first 700 million years.

Earth's Layers

Earth is made up of three main layers: the core, mantle, and crust. The core consists of a solid inner core and a liquid outer core. The inner core, 1.5 percent of Earth's total mass, is made of solid iron and nickel. It is extremely hot, but the enormous pressure from surrounding layers prevents it from melting. The pressure at the center of Earth is 3.7 million times greater than the pressure at

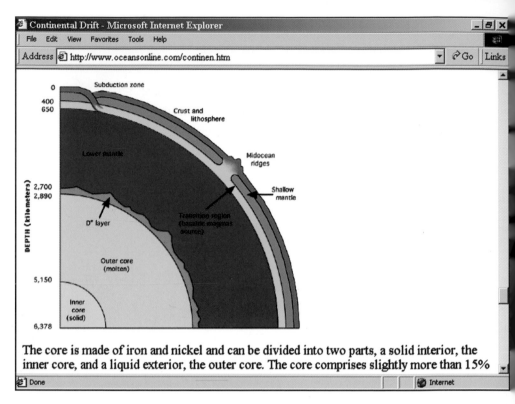

Continental Drift - Microsoft Internet Explorer

File   Edit   View   Favorites   Tools   Help

Address http://www.oceansonline.com/continen.htm   Go   Links

DEPTH (kilometers)

0
400
650

Subduction zone

Crust and
lithosphere

Lower mantle

Midocean
ridges

Shallow
mantle

2,700
2,890

D" layer

Transition region
(basaltic magmas
source)

Outer core
(molten)

5,150

Inner
core
(solid)

6,378

The core is made of iron and nickel and can be divided into two parts, a solid interior, the inner core, and a liquid exterior, the outer core. The core comprises slightly more than 15%

Done   Internet

This diagram illustrates the layers of Earth, from its inner core to its lithosphere, which is made up of the crust and outermost part of the mantle.

the planet's surface. Earth's outer core, 30 percent of Earth's mass, is made of molten, or liquid, iron and nickel. Earth's outer core is subjected to less pressure, so its 7,400°F (4,093°C) temperature keeps it liquid. Scientists believe that Earth's strong magnetic field is generated by electrical currents in this liquid outer core.

The mantle, which makes up 67 percent of Earth's mass, lies between the core and the crust. Most of the mantle is dense, solid rock made of iron, magnesium, aluminum, silicon, silicon compounds, and oxygen.

The crust is less than one percent of Earth's mass. Made of rock and soil, it rests on the mantle. The crust is very thin. According to planetary geologist Thomas R. Watters, the crust "is proportionately as thin as the skin of an apple in relation to the diameter of Earth."[1] Although it is relatively thin, the crust nevertheless includes Earth's highest mountains, deepest canyons, and the oceans and ocean floors.

The crust and the outermost part of the mantle also form a layer called the lithosphere, which is made up of interlocking plates. These plates are large slabs of solid rock that float on and travel over the mantle. The continents and ocean floors, part of the crust, are embedded in the constantly moving plates of the lithosphere.

Shift and Drift

The movement and interaction of these plates is a process known as plate tectonics, based on the theory of plate tectonics, which has existed for fewer than fifty years. (The word *tectonic* comes

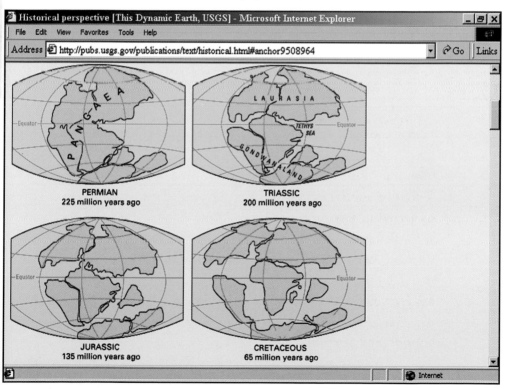

▲ Scientists believe that Earth's seven continents were once part of a huge "supercontinent" known as Pangaea. These maps show how the continents have drifted apart over 225 million years.

from the Greek root "to build.") Geologists, scientists who study Earth, now believe that plate movement of one kind or another plays a large role in the resurfacing of Earth. The movement of the plates is responsible for earthquakes and volcanoes, and it is also responsible for continental drift.

Long ago in Earth's history—about 500 million years ago—there were just two giant continents—Laurasia to the north and Gondwanaland to the south. These two continents slowly merged into one huge supercontinent, known as Pangaea (from the Greek *pan,* "all" and *gaea,* "lands.") Surrounding Pangaea was the vast ocean known as Panthalassa, also from the Greek, meaning "all the seas."

About 200 million years ago, the supercontinent, driven by movement of the plates, began breaking apart. Pangaea again split into Laurasia and Gondwanaland. Then Laurasia broke apart into North America and Eurasia, while Gondwanaland became Africa, South America, India, Australia, and Antarctica. The continents have slowly drifted to their present positions. But as the plates continue to move, continental drift is still occurring. Today the Atlantic Ocean is growing wider by a few inches each year, and the Pacific Ocean is slowly shrinking by the same amount.

▶ Wegener's Theory

In 1915, German meteorologist Alfred Wegener became the first scientist to propose a theory of continental drift. He noticed that the west coast of Africa looked as though it fit neatly into the east coast of South America, like pieces of a jigsaw puzzle. Wegener was not the first to notice the matching shape of these two coasts. Three centuries earlier, English philosopher Francis Bacon studied the first crudely drawn maps of the world and wrote in *Novum Organum* that the similarity of the coasts of Africa and South America could not merely be an accident.

Wegener also discovered that layers of rock, or strata, that matched each other, as well as matching fossil evidence, could be found on both sides of the Atlantic Ocean. These findings convinced him that the continents must have been joined at one time and then drifted apart. In 1915, Wegener published his ideas in *The Origin of Continents and Oceans*. But Wegener had no idea how the continents could have moved. It was not until the 1960s that geologists began to understand the process of plate tectonics.

Earthquakes and Volcanoes

Earth's plates sometimes collide with each other and sometimes slide past each other as they move both vertically and horizontally. In California, for example, there are plates—the Pacific Plate and the North American Plate—that slide by each other, and it is at this

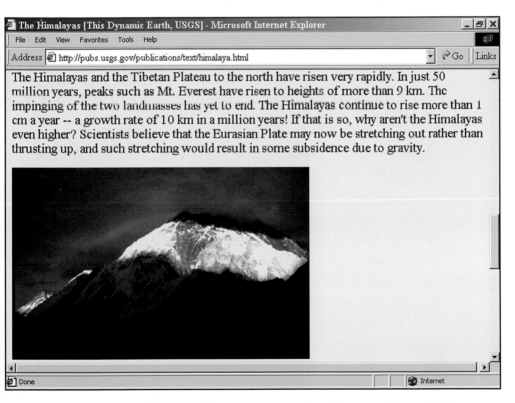

The Himalayas [This Dynamic Earth, USGS] - Microsoft Internet Explorer

File   Edit   View   Favorites   Tools   Help

Address http://pubs.usgs.gov/publications/text/himalaya.html   Go   Links

The Himalayas and the Tibetan Plateau to the north have risen very rapidly. In just 50 million years, peaks such as Mt. Everest have risen to heights of more than 9 km. The impinging of the two landmasses has yet to end. The Himalayas continue to rise more than 1 cm a year -- a growth rate of 10 km in a million years! If that is so, why aren't the Himalayas even higher? Scientists believe that the Eurasian Plate may now be stretching out rather than thrusting up, and such stretching would result in some subsidence due to gravity.

Done   Internet

A sunset view of snowcapped Mount Everest, the tallest mountain on Earth, which rises nearly thirty thousand feet in the Himalayas. The first people to climb to the mountain's summit achieved that feat in 1953. Fifty years later, the mountain is suffering the consequences of tourism and global climate change.

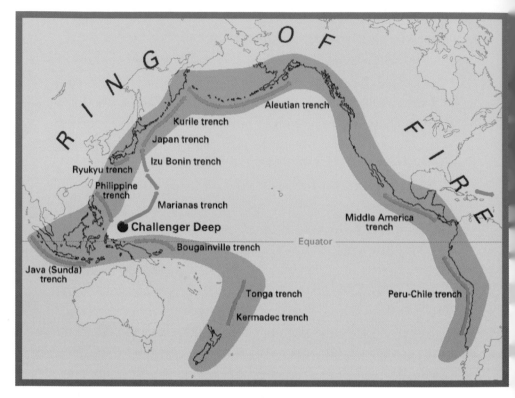

▲ *More than half of Earth's active volcanoes above sea level are found in the Ring of Fire, an area of volcanic arcs and ocean trenches found in the Pacific Ocean basin. It is also an earthquake zone.*

point where earthquakes occur. The San Andreas earthquake fault in California runs along the boundary of these two plates. Often the plates do not slip by each other smoothly because friction holds the upper layers of crust together. But the plates continue to move, and pressure builds up on the surface. Finally, when the strain has more force than the friction can hold, the plates slip. An earthquake occurs as the resulting movement sends shock waves through Earth.

When plates collide with each other, mountain ranges are sometimes formed. This type of collision actually occurs in extreme slow motion—the plates move only a couple of inches a year. India's collision with central Asia to the north resulted in the creation of the Himalayas, home to the highest mountain on Earth, Mount Everest.[2]

The movement and pressure within Earth are also responsible for volcanoes. There are more than five hundred active volcanoes on Earth. They form when molten rock called magma rises from the mantle through the crust. The magma, called lava when it reaches the surface, comes up through vents. Over time, the lava from a volcanic eruption builds up and creates a mountain.

Some volcanoes occur at the boundaries of plates. Most volcanoes are in this category. Many of these, such as the Cascade Mountains in the Pacific Northwest, are at the edges of the Pacific Plate and form the "Ring of Fire," an area of earthquakes and volcanic activity circling the Pacific Ocean. On May 18, 1980, the top 1,312 feet (400 meters) of Washington State's Mount St. Helens was blasted away in a violent volcanic eruption.

Other volcanoes occur in the interior of plates and still others occur at mid-ocean ridges on the ocean floor. The mid-ocean ridges are actually huge mountain ranges that run down the middle of the major oceans. Lava erupts and then cools and hardens to form new seafloor, which eventually pushes outward away from the ridge. Ocean-ridge volcanic eruptions can form islands, such as the Hawaiian Islands.

Chapter 3

Earth's Oceans and Atmosphere

Oceans cover more than 70 percent of Earth's surface and make up 97 percent of Earth's water. But when Earth formed, there were no oceans, at least no oceans consisting of water. The infant Earth was, however, completely covered by an ocean of molten rock many miles deep. In those days, Earth was constantly bombarded by meteors and asteroids—the rocky bodies left over from the creation of the solar system. This bombardment generated enough heat to keep Earth's surface molten for hundreds of millions of years.

▶ Water World

The bombardment of Earth began to slow, as the numbers of asteroids and meteors in the solar system steadily decreased. As Earth began to cool, a thin crust formed on the molten surface. In Earth's infancy, it was molten not just on the surface but all the way through to the solid core, where water was mixed in with the minerals. During volcanic eruptions, water was released from these minerals as steam and then cooled to form clouds. Torrential rains fell from these cooling clouds. Low places in the crust filled with water, forming lakes. As the rains continued, Earth's surface was soon covered by an ocean—a two-mile-deep world ocean.

Scientists believe that when Earth's first ocean formed, it may have only lasted until the next large asteroid or comet struck our planet and generated enough heat to boil away the ocean. Then Earth cooled once again, and a new ocean formed. The process may have been repeated several times. Ocean-boiling events ended about 3.9 billion years ago. Eventually, the world ocean

▲ *This coral looks as if it came from the Moon, but it makes its home in Earth's oceans. The skeletons of these marine animals build upon each other, forming coral reefs that protect coastal regions on Earth.*

was broken by dry land as the process of plate tectonics began. Heat and pressure inside Earth created rock lighter than the ocean floor. This lighter material became the continents that were embedded in the plates that floated on the mantle.

Today, Earth still has a world ocean. Although we give names to separate oceans—the Atlantic, Pacific, Indian, Arctic, and Antarctic, or Southern—all of Earth's oceans are connected and make up one large body of water. The average depth of all the oceans is about 12,000 feet (3,700 meters). The deepest spot in the world's oceans is found in the Pacific Ocean. The Mariana Trench near Japan is 36,198 feet (11,033 meters) deep.

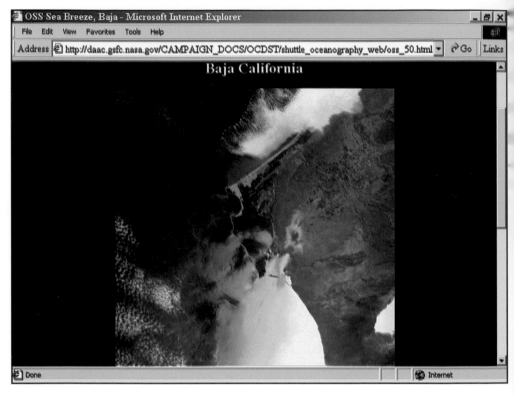

OSS Sea Breeze, Baja - Microsoft Internet Explorer

File   Edit   View   Favorites   Tools   Help

Address   http://daac.gsfc.nasa.gov/CAMPAIGN_DOCS/OCDST/shuttle_oceanography_web/oss_50.html   Go   Links

Baja California

▲ *Felt but rarely seen, a sea breeze is photographed over Baja California, Mexico, by the crew of the space shuttle* Columbia *in 1981. Meteorologists have since learned that localized sea breezes such as this one are typical of many coasts.*

▷ The Changing Atmosphere

Scientists believe that Earth's first atmosphere consisted mainly of hydrogen gas, with little or no oxygen. The Mars-size asteroid that scientists think created the Moon probably destroyed this atmosphere. That collision may have resulted in a temporary atmosphere of hot, vaporized metal. Then came a long period of massive volcanic eruptions all over Earth. The volcanoes poured enormous amounts of carbon dioxide and water vapor into the sky, forming an atmosphere much more dense than today's atmosphere. How did our atmosphere thin out, then? Water vapor cooled to form rain, and rain formed the oceans. Carbon dioxide dissolved into rain and the oceans. Plants removed carbon dioxide from the air and released oxygen.

When life began on Earth, it brought about drastic changes to the atmosphere. As life continued to evolve, it affected and was affected by the atmosphere. Today's atmosphere is about 78 percent nitrogen, 20 percent oxygen, 1 percent argon, and 1 percent water vapor.[1]

The Structure of Earth's Atmosphere

The blanket of air that is Earth's atmosphere absorbs the Sun's energy, recycles water and other chemicals, and works with electrical and magnetic forces to give us a moderate climate that supports life. Our atmosphere is divided into four layers: the troposphere, stratosphere, mesosphere, and thermosphere.

The layer closest to the ground is the troposphere, which extends up to about 7 miles (11 kilometers). Almost all of Earth's weather happens here because constant movement of the air in this layer guarantees that conditions are always changing. The air in the troposphere is usually warmest near the ground and coolest near the upper boundary since the ground absorbs sunlight and heats the air.

The next layer is the stratosphere, extending to a height of about 30 miles (50 kilometers). Inside the stratosphere is a layer of ozone, which absorbs most of the Sun's harmful ultraviolet light, keeping it from reaching Earth's surface. Air temperatures in the stratosphere range from −76°F (−60°C) at the bottom to 50°F (10°C) at the top.

Above the stratosphere is the mesosphere, extending upward to about 50 miles (80 kilometers). The air in the mesosphere is too thin to absorb much heat, so temperatures fall to −135°F (−93°C) at the top of this layer.

The fourth layer, the thermosphere, rises to a height of about 400 miles (640 kilometers) above the mesosphere. This layer is extremely hot due to the ultraviolet radiation from the Sun that it absorbs. Temperatures at the upper boundary can reach

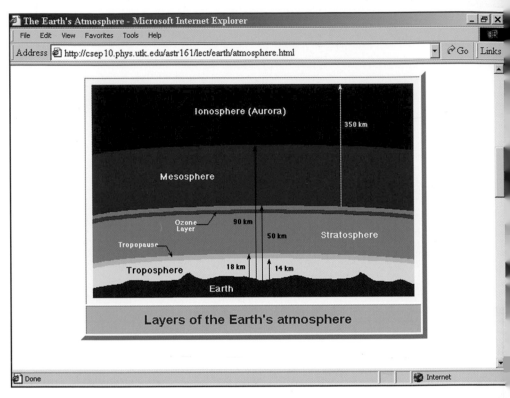

The Earth's Atmosphere - Microsoft Internet Explorer

File   Edit   View   Favorites   Tools   Help

Address http://csep10.phys.utk.edu/astr161/lect/earth/atmosphere.html   Go   Links

Ionosphere (Aurora)   350 km

Mesosphere

Ozone
Layer   90 km
                                    50 km   Stratosphere
Tropopause

Troposphere   18 km   14 km

Earth

Layers of the Earth's atmosphere

Done   Internet

⚠ *Earth's atmosphere is usually divided into four layers, as seen in this diagram.*

3,600°F (1,982°C). Electrically charged particles from the Sun cause molecules of gas to glow in this layer, resulting in the shimmering bands and curtains of color in Earth's skies known as aurorae (named for Aurora, the Roman goddess of dawn). The aurora borealis, or the northern lights, can be seen in Earth's Northern Hemisphere while the aurora australis, or the southern lights, can be seen in the Southern Hemisphere.

The ionosphere, the upper part of the thermosphere, is made of gas particles that are ionized, or electrically charged, by the Sun's ultraviolet radiation. These electrically charged particles play an important role in telecommunications by reflecting radio signals, allowing them to be bounced around Earth.

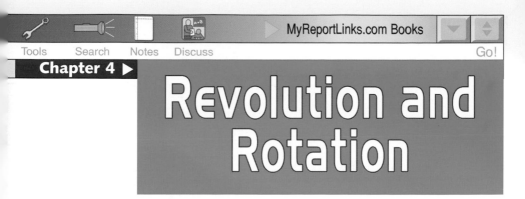
Revolution and Rotation

Planet Earth is constantly moving. It makes one complete revolution, or orbit, around the Sun in 365 1/4 days, or one year. Although our calendar shows a year as consisting of 365 days, we add an extra day, February 29, every four years to account for the extra quarter day each year.

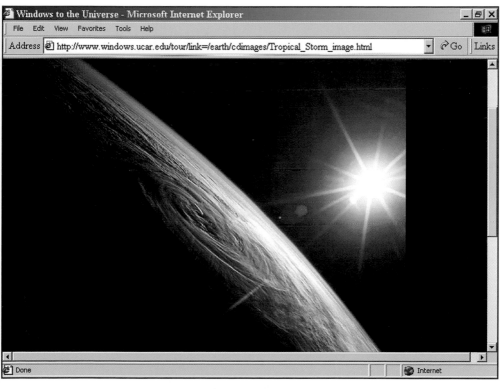

▲ Earth orbits the Sun at a speed of roughly 67,000 miles per hour. The swirling surface seen on this sunlit photograph of Earth is a tropical storm.

Earth's average distance from the Sun is about 93 million miles (150 million kilometers). Earth's orbit is not a perfect circle but an ellipse, so Earth's distance from the Sun varies. The ancients who believed in a motionless Earth would have been amazed to learn that throughout the year, Earth hurtles along its orbit around the Sun at about 67,000 miles per hour.[1]

The Spinning Earth

As Earth revolves around the Sun, it also spins or rotates on its axis, an imaginary line running from the North Pole through the center of the planet to the South Pole. This spinning or rotation is what gives us night and day. Earth spins at over 500 miles per hour (804 kilometers per hour), and one complete rotation takes one day—24 hours (23 hours 56 minutes, to be exact). The side of Earth that faces the Sun experiences daytime while the side of Earth that is turned away from the Sun experiences nighttime. When seen from the North Pole, Earth rotates counterclockwise, which is why the Sun appears to rise in the east and set in the west.

A day on Earth was not always 24 hours. In Earth's distant past, when the Moon was created, a day was only about five or six hours long. But over time, the powerful gravitational pull of the Moon on the tides in Earth's oceans caused a gradual slowing of Earth's rotation and an increase in the length of the day. Earth's rotation is still slowing.

Earth's rotation also affects the circulation of air around the planet as well as currents in the ocean. The tendency of warm air to rise and cold air to fall sets in motion a global pattern of winds. Warm air at the equator rises and moves toward the poles, while cold air from the poles moves toward the equator. The cooler air replaces the rising warm air. Earth's rotation affects the movement of air by deflecting winds to the right in the Northern Hemisphere and to the left in the Southern Hemisphere. This process, known as the Coriolis effect, breaks up the big wind system into several smaller circular wind systems.

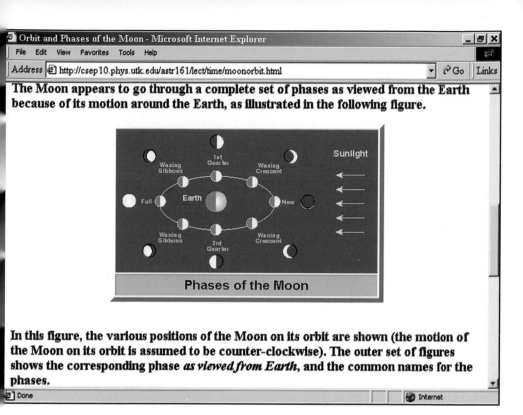

The Moon appears to go through a complete set of phases as viewed from the Earth because of its motion around the Earth, as illustrated in the following figure.

In this figure, the various positions of the Moon on its orbit are shown (the motion of the Moon on its orbit is assumed to be counter-clockwise). The outer set of figures shows the corresponding phase *as viewed from Earth*, and the common names for the phases.

▲ Because of its motion around Earth, the Moon when viewed from Earth appears to go through phases.

▷ The Moon and Tides

Tides are temporary shifts in water levels along the ocean shores. Earth's tides are caused by the Moon's gravity pulling on the oceans. As the Moon travels in its orbit around Earth, its gravity causes our oceans to bulge on the side of Earth that faces the Moon. The force of Earth's rotation causes another bulge in the oceans on the side of Earth that is away from the Moon. These bulges in the oceans are high tides, while the areas between these bulges are low tides. Ocean waters on Earth rise and fall in tides twice a day.

Twice a month, the Sun and Moon lie in a straight line with Earth. This alignment results in an especially strong gravitational

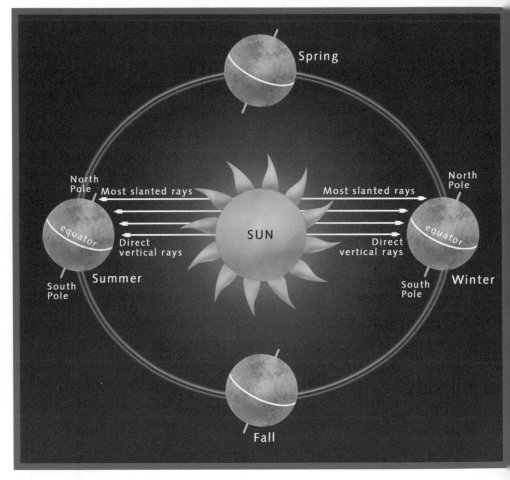

The changes in seasons on Earth are caused by the tilt in Earth's axis. This diagram in which Earth is seen revolving around the Sun shows the seasons of the Northern Hemisphere.

pull. At such times, the tides, known as spring tides (which have no connection to the season of the same name), are especially high and low. Also twice a month, the Sun and the Moon form a right angle with Earth. This causes the Sun's gravitational pull to work against the Moon's pull, which results in neap tides. Neap tides are neither very high nor very low.

The Four Seasons

Earth's axis is tilted at an angle of 23.5 degrees. This tilt causes two things to change as Earth revolves around the Sun during the year—the angle at which the Sun's rays strike Earth and the number of hours of daylight. It is the tilt of Earth's axis and not a change in Earth's distance from the Sun that is responsible for the change of seasons.

When the North Pole is tipped away from the Sun, it is winter in the Northern Hemisphere and summer in the Southern Hemisphere. The sun's rays reach the Northern Hemisphere at a greater angle and are weaker than the more direct rays striking the Southern Hemisphere. Since there is less sunlight during the winter, there is less heat absorbed by the ground. When the North Pole is tipped toward the Sun, it is summer in the Northern Hemisphere and winter in the Southern Hemisphere. Since there is more daylight during the summer, the ground absorbs more heat each hour.

As Earth journeys around the Sun each year, the length of the days changes. In the Northern Hemisphere, the longest day of the year is known as the summer solstice. It occurs on about June 20. The autumnal equinox occurs on about September 22, when the day and night are the same length. The winter solstice, the shortest day of the year, occurs on about December 21. And on about March 20, which is the vernal equinox, day and night are again the same length.

Daylight hours vary the most the closer you are to either of the poles. During the winter, the hours of daylight decrease as you approach the poles. At the poles, the sun never rises above the horizon in winter and never sets during the summer. The equator, the imaginary line that circles Earth, gets about twelve hours of daylight throughout the year.

Life on Earth

The earliest life on Earth was much different than it is today. Human beings could not have breathed the atmosphere at that time. But over millions of years, changing conditions permitted new and more complex forms of life to evolve, which finally resulted in plants, animals, and human beings.

▷ All the Right Ingredients for Life

Scientists do not know how life first arose on Earth. But they believe Earth contained all the necessary ingredients to make the emergence of life possible. The early ocean was lifeless and contained huge amounts of carbon dioxide. One of the elements of carbon dioxide is carbon. A carbon-based molecule has the ability to split into two identical halves, reproducing itself. When the first continents formed, minerals and chemical elements were washed into the ocean by rains and tides. Energy from the Sun, lightning, and tides combined to affect these minerals and chemicals.

The billions of carbon-based molecules in the oceans eventually evolved into the first living cells. Scientists have found fossils of primitive bacteria cells in 3.5-billion-year-old rocks in South Africa and Australia. These fossil cells, probably the earliest forms of life on Earth, have the same shapes as today's bacteria—rods, balls, and spirals.

Simple plantlike bacteria called blue-green algae formed colonies of floating mats on the sea. The algae broke down carbon dioxide in the atmosphere and released oxygen into the air. About 2.2 billion years ago, this oxygen began to replace much of the carbon dioxide in the atmosphere. Oxygen was poisonous to

▲ *This photograph of Earth's Western Hemisphere was taken by a NOAA weather satellite in 1992. It shows Hurricane Andrew, one of the deadliest hurricanes to strike the United States, making landfall on the Louisiana coast.*

blue-green algae, but it was essential in Earth's atmosphere. It allowed the creation of the ozone layer, which was needed to protect future life on Earth from the Sun's ultraviolet radiation.

As oxygen slowly replaced carbon dioxide in the atmosphere, new types of cells were evolving in the ocean. Unlike blue-green algae and other early forms of bacteria, these cells contained their

Pictured is a trilobite fossil from Morocco. Trilobites, early marine animals now extinct, were related to horseshoe crabs and spiders and were the first animals on Earth to have eyes.

DNA, or genetic material, within a nucleus, an inner structure protected by a membrane. These cells eventually evolved into protozoa, tiny one-celled organisms that are the ancestors of animals, and another type of algae, which was the ancestor of plants.

Life Explodes: Plants and Animals Emerge

About 600 million years ago, Earth underwent a rapid change. The oceans became filled with many different forms of life. About 500 million years ago, creatures known as trilobites were common. Trilobites were invertebrates, animals without backbones. These sea animals are now extinct, but we know about them through their fossil remains. More than four thousand species of trilobites have been identified from the fossil record. Then the first vertebrates, or animals with backbones, appeared. (Mammals, birds, reptiles, and fishes are all vertebrates.)

About 400 million years ago, the first plants and animals emerged on land. Large ocean tides created tidal zones that were alternately wet and dry, which made it possible for animals to move from the sea to the land. A species of fish called lungfish was able to exist on land and in water. Once animals and plants emerged from water, they had to adapt to survive on land. They needed to breathe and find ways to avoid drying out and becoming overheated in the sun. The first trees, the first flying insects, and the first amphibians appeared. Reptiles appeared next, and then came mammals and birds.

The Human Animal

In 2004, there were more than 6.4 billion people living on Earth, according to the World Population Clock of the United States Census Bureau, which estimates the worldwide population. As different as modern humans are in race, nationality, custom, and religious belief, we are all part of the same species: *Homo sapiens.*

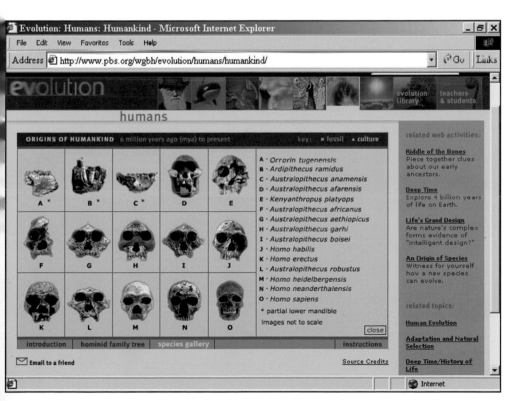

▲ Humans have changed over time, as this chart of human skeletal remains shows.

Scientists recognize about fifteen different species of early human, although they disagree on how these early humans are related. But scientific evidence does show that the physical and behavioral traits shared by all people began with our apelike ancestors who lived between 5 million and 8 million years ago.[1] The earliest records we have of our modern human species, *Homo sapiens,* shows that humans appeared a few million years ago in Africa. From there they migrated to Asia and later to Europe, probably within the past million years.[2]

▶ Biomes and the Diversity of Life

When humans emerged, they became part of complex ecosystems that were developing on Earth. In these ecosystems, all forms of life interacted with one another and depended on one another and their environment. Within these ecosystems are communities of plants and animals that live in certain climates, and these are

▲ *Earth is home to vastly different land and climate regions known as biomes. At left, Monument Valley in Arizona is part of a desert biome, while northern British Columbia's evergreen forests (above) are prime examples of the taiga, or boreal forest.*

known as biomes. Today there are seven main biomes on Earth: tropical rain forest, desert, chaparral, temperate forest, grasslands, taiga, and tundra.

Tropical rain forest biomes are found near the equator in areas where rain falls every day. Tall rain forest trees form a dense canopy, the uppermost layer of branches in the forest. In the canopy live monkeys, flying squirrels, bats, and sloths.

Desert biomes are areas with very little rainfall. Most deserts support animals, such as Gila monsters, that have adapted to the dry conditions. Many desert plants are succulents—plants with fleshy fat leaves, such as cactuses, that absorb and store water.

Chaparral biomes are areas that have rainy winter seasons followed by summer drought. Chaparral plants include scrub oak, manzanita, and others adapted to dry conditions. Animals that live there include skunks, mice, and deer. A variety of reptiles and birds can also be found in the chaparral.

Temperate forest biomes have frequent rain and cold winters. The forests consist mainly of deciduous trees, which are trees that shed their leaves each autumn. Inhabitants of temperate forests include birds, small mammals, deer, black bears, wolves, and a variety of insects, worms, and spiders.

Grassland biomes occur in areas that experience long, dry periods. Occasional fires in grasslands prevent the growth of large trees and shrubs. Grassland inhabitants include grazing animals such as bison and burrowing animals such as prairie dogs.

The taiga biome is at the northern end of the temperate zone. Taiga winters are long and cold, and taiga summers are short. Trees that grow in this area are mainly conifers, evergreen trees with cones, such as pine trees. Moose, elk, black bears, and lynxes can be found in the taiga.

Tundra biomes are mainly in the far north but can also be found on very high mountains where severe cold persists through much of the year. Soil in the tundra is permanently frozen except for a thin layer that thaws briefly each summer. Typical tundra plant life consists of lichens, mosses, and a few grasses and shrubs. Musk ox, caribou, reindeer, and Arctic wolves can be found in the northern tundra.

▶ Life in and on the Water

The largest biomes are those in Earth's waters. Marine biomes are saltwater ecosystems that are found at different depths of the ocean as well as in estuaries, shallow areas where freshwater and salt water mix. Freshwater biomes include wetlands such as swamps, marshes, and bogs; areas of moving water such as rivers and streams; and areas of standing water, such as ponds and lakes.

Plants, animals, and their environments on Earth continue to interact and depend on one another for survival. They have survived for millions of years because green plants give off oxygen,

▲ *A lone figure is dwarfed by an iceberg in Canada's Northwest Territories. Earth has experienced periods known as ice ages more than once in its history, and will undoubtedly enter a new ice age in the future.*

which animals need to breathe, and animals breathe out carbon dioxide, which plants need. These processes have kept the oxygen levels in Earth's atmosphere at about the same levels—about 20 percent—for the past 400 million years.

▶ Gaia, the Living Earth

Earth's atmosphere, climate, and land and sea features have continued to support life over the last several billion years. Unlike Venus, Earth did not become too hot for life, and unlike Mars, it did not grow too cold for life. Instead, Earth has managed to provide a changing atmosphere suited to the millions of different species of animals and plants. But just how has it managed to do this?

In 1979, British scientist James Lovelock proposed a startling explanation—Earth is a living organism. Lovelock called our planet Gaia, after a Greek goddess who drew the living world from chaos.[3] Lovelock's Gaia theory describes Earth as if it were a single living organism that adapts to changes when it needs to. When changes occur in the environment, Earth, or Gaia, automatically adjusts so that there is enough oxygen for animals and carbon dioxide for plants. Although scientists agree that Earth is a complex web of interrelated elements, most scientists do not accept Lovelock's Gaia theory.

Ice Ages and Asteroids

If Gaia existed, though, she would have faced enormous challenges in keeping the flicker of life burning on Earth, which has faced many life-threatening challenges. Our planet has experienced ice ages, periods lasting millions of years, during which glaciers covered much of Earth. The extreme cold made life difficult, and glaciers changed the nature of life itself as organisms had to adapt to new conditions in order to survive. About 2.5 billion years ago, and again between 600 million and 800 million years ago, Earth experienced ice ages so severe that the planet was covered in ice from the North Pole to the South Pole. Only the hardiest forms of life could have survived these events, which scientists refer to as "Snowball Earth."[4]

Scientists do not know for certain what caused Earth's ice ages, but they have several theories. Carbon dioxide and water vapor are powerful greenhouse agents that trap solar heat, keeping Earth warm enough to sustain life. It is possible that during periods of low levels of carbon dioxide in the atmosphere, Earth enters an ice age. Some believe that continental drift can trigger an ice age. When continents move toward the poles, thick ice sheets form. Others believe that changes in ocean circulation can bring on an ice age. Then there are those who point to changes in Earth's orbit around the Sun and slight variations in the tilt of Earth's axis. Each of these factors may result in a cooling of Earth because they influence how much sunlight strikes the planet. Recently, a physicist at the University of California at Berkeley

Millions of Earth's animal species have gone extinct. The koala, native to Australia, is one species that faces the danger of extinction. Each species that leaves the Earth permanently affects all other species on our planet.

pointed out that roughly every 100,000 years, Earth passes through a "ring of cosmic debris and dust" that may block enough sunlight to trigger an ice age.[5]

There have been events in Earth's history even more catastrophic than ice ages, however. On repeated occasions, Earth has been struck by huge asteroids and comets. These killer asteroids are believed to be responsible for several mass extinctions. About 250 million years ago, 95 percent of all the living things on Earth suddenly died, and scientists believe a large asteroid or comet striking Earth was the most likely cause of their deaths. About 66 million years ago, an asteroid slammed into the region of what is now Yucatán, Mexico, forming a crater more than 100 miles (160 kilometers) wide. That crater is known as Chicxulub Crater.[6] When this asteroid struck Earth, more than 75 percent of Earth's plant and animal life, including the dinosaurs, were killed. But as Earth had already shown, its life proved to be resilient, and the disappearance of the dinosaurs made way for a new age of mammals, which eventually included humans. So, according to some, the human race owes its existence to a killer asteroid!

The Future of Earth

The challenge facing us today is that our very presence on this planet threatens the continued existence of life on Earth. The living organisms around the world may simply not be able to adapt to all the environmental changes brought about by human beings. Paleontologist David Raup has calculated that during the past 500 million years, one species on Earth, on average, has gone extinct every four or five years. In contrast, biologist Paul Ehrlich believes that the current extinction rates are measurable in species disappearing from Earth by the hour.[7] And when one species goes extinct, all other species in an ecosystem are affected by its removal.

Human beings are contributing to an overall warming of Earth by the constant burning of fossil fuels such as oil, gas, and coal. Such activity adds carbon dioxide to the atmosphere, which in turn strengthens the greenhouse effect. Nearly all scientists agree that global warming will bring about unpredictable changes in climate that will almost certainly result in unpleasant consequences in at least some parts of the world. As ice melts in the polar regions, the sea level around the world will rise, which will drown some islands and the low coastal areas of many continents.

Other scientists believe that melting ice in the Arctic Ocean could actually trigger a new ice age by affecting the Gulf Stream, the ocean current that moderates the climate in the northeastern United States, eastern Canada, and western and northern Europe. Without the moderating effect of the Gulf Stream, these places would face the beginning of a climate like that of Siberia. According to scientists, this kind of change has happened several times, and the change could take place quickly—in a decade or even in as little as two or three years![8]

Nobody can accurately predict Earth's future, but we can be sure of one thing: Earth, our home, is a planet of constant change, and its plants, animals, and people have made amazing adaptations to those changes over time in order to survive.

carbon dioxide—A gas made up of carbon and oxygen that humans exhale and plants take in.

continental drift—The theory or process of the continents on Earth drifting because of the movement of Earth's plates.

DNA—Deoxyribonucleic acid, which is the essential part of all living matter and is the basic material found in cells. DNA carries the materials that are inherited from one generation to the next.

elliptical—Shaped like an ellipse, or oval. Earth's orbit is elliptical.

equinox—Two times in the year when the Sun crosses the equator; the vernal equinox ushers in spring, and the autumnal equinox, fall.

extinct organism—A form of life that no longer exists.

meteorology—The branch of science that studies Earth's weather, climate, and atmosphere.

organism—An individual living thing.

ozone layer—A layer in Earth's atmosphere that protects Earth from damaging ultraviolet radiation; ozone is a form of oxygen gas.

plate tectonics—The movement and interaction of large slabs of Earth's crust, known as plates.

solstice—Two times in the year when the Sun reaches either farthest north of the equator or farthest south of the equator; in the Northern Hemisphere, the summer solstice marks the beginning of summer, and the winter solstice marks the beginning of winter.

ultraviolet radiation—Invisible rays of light from the Sun that, depending on their strength, both benefit and harm living things on Earth.

Chapter 1. The Home Planet

1. Peter D.Ward and Donald Brownlee, *The Life and Death of Planet Earth* (New York: Times Books, 2003), p. 75.

2. Carl Sagan, *Cosmos* (New York: Random House, 1980), pp. 51–52.

Chapter 2. A Planet of Constant Change

1. Thomas R. Watters, *Planets: A Smithsonian Guide* (New York: Macmillan, 1995), p. 74.

2. Peter D.Ward and Donald Brownlee, *The Life and Death of Planet Earth* (New York: Times Books, 2003), p. 55.

Chapter 3. Earth's Oceans and Atmosphere

1. Thomas R. Watters, *Planets: A Smithsonian Guide* (New York: Macmillan, 1995), p. 72.

Chapter 4. Revolution and Rotation

1. Laboratory for High Energy Astrophysics at the Goddard Space Flight Center, NASA, "Imagine the Universe: Speed of the Earth's Rotation," n.d., <http://imagine.gsfc.nasa.gov/docs/ask_astro/answers/970401c.html> (July 12, 2004).

Chapter 5. Life on Earth

1. Smithsonian National Museum of Natural History, The Human Origins Program, *Research Guide to Paleoanthropology*, "Human Evolution," n.d., <http://www.mnh.si.edu/anthro/humanorigins/faq/Encarta/encarta.htm> (June 30, 2004).

2. Ibid.

3. Peter D. Ward and Donald Brownlee, *The Life and Death of Planet Earth* (New York: Times Books, 2003), p. 52.

4. Ibid., p. 75.

5. Ibid., p. 81.

6. Thomas R. Watters, *Planets: A Smithsonian Guide* (New York: Macmillan, 1995), p. 89.

7. Ward and Brownlee, p. 45.

8. Thom Hartmann, "How Global Warming May Cause the Next Ice Age," adapted from *The Last Hours of Ancient Sunlight* by Thom Hartmann (New York: Random House, 2004).

Further Reading

Asimov, Isaac, with revisions and updating by Richard Hantula. *Earth*. Milwaukee: Gareth Stevens, 2002.

Cole, Michael D. *Earth—The Third Planet*. Berkeley Heights, N.J.: Enslow Publishers, Inc., 2001.

Downs, Sandra. *When the Earth Moves*. Brookfield, Conn.: Twenty-First Century Books, 2000.

Gallant, Roy A. *Dance of the Continents*. New York: Benchmark Books, 2000.

Johansson, Philip. *The Temperate Forest*. Berkeley Heights, N.J.: Enslow Publishers, Inc., 2004.

———. *The Tropical Rain Forest*. Berkeley Heights, N.J.: Enslow Publishers, Inc., 2004.

Miller, Ron. *Earth and the Moon*. Brookfield, Conn.: Twenty-First Century Books, 2003.

Munro, Margaret. *The Story of Life on Earth*. Vancouver: Douglas & McIntyre, 2000.

Patent, Dorothy Hinshaw. *Shaping the Earth*. New York: Clarion Books, 2000.

Spangenburg, Ray, and Kit Moser. *If an Asteroid Hit Earth*. New York: Franklin Watts, 2000.

Stefoff, Rebecca. *Earth and the Moon*. New York: Benchmark Books, 2002.

Tabak, John. *A Look at Earth*. New York: Franklin Watts, 2003.

A

amphibians, 37
Aristarchus, 12–14
asteroids, 24, 26, 43
Atlantic Ocean, 20, 25
atmosphere, 10, 15, 17, 26–28, 34–35, 41–42, 44
aurora, 28
autumnal equinox, 33

B

bacteria, 34–35
biomes, 38–40
birds, 36–37, 40
blue-green algae, 34–35

C

carbon dioxide, 17, 26–27, 34–35, 41–42, 44
Chicxulub Crater, 43
comets, 24, 43
continental drift, 20–21
continents, 15, 19–21, 25, 34, 42, 44
Copernicus, Nicolaus, 14
core, 16–19
crust, 17–19, 22, 24

D

dinosaurs, 43
DNA, 36

E

Earth, bombardment of, 17, 24
earthquakes, 15, 21–23
ecosystems, 38, 40, 44

F

fossils, 34, 36

G

Gaia theory, 41–42
glaciers, 15, 42
global warming, 44
gravitational pull, 16, 30–32
greenhouse effect, 44
Gulf Stream, 44

H

Homo sapiens, 37–38

I

ice ages, 42–44

K

Kepler, Johannes, 13–14

L

Lovelock, James, 41–42
lungfish, 36

M

magnetic field, 18
mammals, 36–37, 43
mantle, 17–19, 25
mass extinctions, 43
meteors, 24
Moon, 11–13, 17, 26, 30–32

N

nitrogen, 17, 27

O

orbit, 29–30
oxygen, 27, 34–35, 40
ozone layer, 27

P

Pacific Ocean, 23, 25
plants, 34, 36, 38–41, 43, 44
plates, 19–23
plate tectonics, 19–23, 25
protozoa, 36

R

reptiles, 36–37, 40
revolution, 29
rotation, 30–31

S

seasons, 32–33
solar system, 11, 13, 16
summer solstice, 33
Sun, 10, 12–14, 16, 27, 29–33, 42

T

tides, 30–32, 34, 36
trilobites, 36

U

ultraviolet radiation, 27–28, 35

V

Venus, 10–11, 14, 41
vernal equinox, 33
vertebrates, 36
volcanoes, 15, 20, 21–23, 26

W

Wegener, Alfred, 20–21
winter solstice, 33
world ocean, 24–25